Old Yetholm, Morebattle, Hownam and I

by Roy G. Perkins

A view of Town Yetholm Green, probably taken in the 1920s, looking from High Street towards Cheviot Place and Morebattle. On the left is the Plough Hotel which remains open today. The White Swan Hotel, which is shown on the Ordnance Survey map of 1863 as the Swan Hotel, closed around 1960.

Text © Roy G. Perkins, 2007.
First published in the United Kingdom, 2007,
by Stenlake Publishing Ltd.
www.stenlake.co.uk
ISBN 9781840332940

Acknowledgements

I should like to take this opportunity to thank Mr Brian Ashby of Town Yetholm for his help in the writing of this book and the trouble he went to assist me; Mr John Eagan of Birkenhead for his help with some of the translations which have been undertaken during research; and finally my late Great Uncle, Thomas Robson of Liddesdale, who imbued me with a deep knowledge of Border lore from an early age. Finally, my thanks must also go to the staff and owners of the Border Hotel who tolerated my vagaries and questions during my visits.

Further Reading

Morebattle Millennium History Group, *Kalewater: A Miscellany*, 1999
Ian MacDougall, *Bondagers*, 2000
Maureen M. Meikle, *A British Frontier*, 2004
Alastair Moffat, *The Borders*, 2002
Donald Omand, *The Borders Book*, 1995

Mr A.V. Tokely, *The Kirk Yetholm Gypsies*, 2002
www.yetholmonline.org.uk
www.morebattle.bordernet.co.uk
www.yetholm.bordernet.co.uk

Attonburn, originally Auldtownburn, was the home of the Kers since at least 1357, although by 1700 the Wanlis, or Wanless, family was in possession. Nowadays it is farmed by Mr and Mrs Symons and is a notable stock-rearing farm with some 370 South Country Cheviot breeding ewes and 750 North Country breeding ewes amongst other stock. The farm covers an area of some 1,500 acres and the main structures of the buildings are unchanged since this photograph was taken about 1910.

INTRODUCTION

The name Yetholm or Zetholm appears to be derived from the Saxon word Zete, meaning gate or gateway, and either ham meaning settlement, or holm being Norse and Old English in origin and meaning flat land by the river. So, we have either the settlement by the gateway or the flatland by the gateway. In either case, gate refers to a passageway or pass through the Cheviot Hills - the Bowmont Water.

The basic economic fabric of the villages in this area has always depended on agriculture, though its worth noting that in 1776, while Galashiels had thirty wool looms, Yetholm had thirty-five. Of course, Yetholm never received the benefit of a railway and became, as a result, something of a backwater despite the existence of a toll road from Kalemouth via Morebattle, and Kirk Yetholm to Kilham. There was an attempt to promote a railway to Yetholm, from the Jedburgh Railway near Nisbet, via Morebattle, but the plan came to nothing.

Over the years Yetholm has produced its share of famous individuals from Jean Gordon, the inspiration for Sir Walter Scott's gypsy Meg Merrilees in his *Waverley* novel *Guy Mannering*, to sculptor Jake Harvey and Admiral-of-the-Fleet Sir Henry Francis Oliver. Yetholm, as the two villages of Kirk and Town are collectively known, is still a popular haunt with walkers not least because of its position at the north end of the Pennine Way and on the route of St Cuthberts Way from Lindisfarne to Melrose. But it is perhaps more famed because of its association with the Gypsies, many descendants of whom remain in the villages.

There were many Gypsy communities in southern Scotland but probably none as well known as that of Kirk Yetholm. How they came to be in Kirk Yetholm is a matter of some dispute. Some say it was the result of the outstanding bravery of a Gypsy called Young who served with Captain David Bennet of Grubet at the Battle of Namur in 1695. In gratitude for Young saving his life, Bennet, a notable local landowner, supposedly built cottages in Kirk Yetholm which he leased to the Gypsies. Others, including R. Murray in his book *Gypsies of the Border* (1875), say that the right to settlement in Yetholm was given by Sir William Bennet of Marlfield in gratitude to one of the Faa family for recovering a valuable horse stolen by some Jacobites during the 1715 rebellion.

Whatever their origins in the vicinity, by the time of *The Statistical Account of Scotland* in 1797 there were 50 in the Yetholm tribe. By 1816 there were 109,

and by the time of the *New Statistical Account* in 1835 about 100. The author of the parish's entry in the *New Statistical Account* was John Baird, minister of Yetholm from 1829 to 1861, and as a result of his interest in the tribe, and the ideas he had earlier presented to the Society for the Reformation of Gypsies in Edinburgh, he was invited to try out his plans for them. Funding was agreed by the Quakers in 1839 and covered such items as the accommodation for Gypsy children left behind while their parents travelled, the costs of their education, and arrangements for funding apprenticeships for boys who wanted to learn a trade. Progress was slow, with only one family leaving their children behind while they travelled that first year and then only when Baird himself agreed to accommodate them. In time other Yetholm residents offered to accommodate the children and by 1841 some 49 Gypsy children were attending the local school. The adult Gypsies, however, proved more stubborn and even as late as 1846 only four families were staying at home. However, by the time Baird died in 1861 there had been a substantial increase in the number of families staying at home, attending the church, and whose children attended the Sunday school. Bairds efforts were no doubt philanthropic and well intentioned, but they led inevitably to the gradual destruction of the local Gypsies' way of life, culture and language, and today little of their society remains.

Queen Esther, the last Gypsy Queen, succeeded to the throne in 1861 and died in 1883. There was then an interregnum until 1898 when a new minister of Yetholm, the Rev. William Carrick Miller, arranged a coronation for Charles Faa-Blythe, Esther's son, by then 70 years old. The coronation owed more to pantomime than Gypsy tradition and was evidently aimed mainly at promoting Yetholm's developing popularity as a tourist centre. Charles's reign was not a long one and his death in 1902 marked the end of this Yetholm tradition, though there are still Gypsy blood lines in the village.

The reader will no doubt be tempted, as was the anonymous writer of the parish's entry in the first *Statistical Account*, to surmise that the name Morebattle commemorates some ancient armed conflict, possibly in connection with the age-old struggle between Scotland and England. In fact, the origin of the name is quite different. Old spellings like Mereboda, Merbotle, Merbotele and Merebotle give clues to the fact that the name derives from two elements - mere', a loch or marsh, and 'botl', a village, clachan or settlement - giving a meaning of the settlement or village, of or by, the loch or marsh. The loch which gave rise to the name is no longer obvious, having been drained in the nineteenth century for the purpose of agricultural improvement. However, there is considerable evidence that in earlier times what is now the Linton Loch extended over much of the valley of the Kale Water and right up to the edges of Morebattle village.

Certainly, there was settlement very early and evidence abounds that at some time in the past the population in the outlying areas was considerably greater than it is today. The first *Statistical Account* records that, 'The several encampments, and rows of stones, called 'tryst stones', are antiquities, probably of the most ancient date in the Parish. Morebattle has always been an agricultural community, its sons and daughters gaining their livelihood from the land, and at no period has there been significant industry beyond this and a little hand-loom weaving.'

The former parish of Mow, or Molle, consisted of the southern part of what is now the parish of Morebattle. Mow or Molle, as names, both appear to be derived from the old British or Brythonic peoples, who inhabited the whole of the Borders in Roman and pre-Roman times, and they describe a rounded hill or hills. Mow is first recorded in the time of the Kingdom of Northumbria, when it became the property of the monastery of Lindisfarne. Later, it went through a succession of ownerships and was mentioned repeatedly throughout the medieval period. When and how the church of Mow and its parish were established are lost in the mists of time, but it was certainly in existence in 1153 when it was gifted by the son of Liulf to the monks of Kelso.

The town of Mow or Molle must have been substantial because the monks of Kelso alone had some fourteen cottages here as well as a malt kiln and a mill, while there were also two towers or peels to protect the district from the marauding English. The Parish of Mow or Molle was united with that of Morebattle prior to December 1635 and annexed by it in 1672, the last minister recorded being Robert Martin who served in 1617/18. The church eventually fell into disrepair and nothing of it or the village now remains, save for some graves in the old graveyard.

The name Mowhaugh seems to have come into more widespread use following the demise of the actual village and means simply the haugh or alluvial flatland of Mow. In 1889 James Tait wrote in his *Two Centuries of Border Church Life* that 'Gone is the ancient town, which, as records say, contained many fair houses. Vanished are the protecting towers, of which two existed here, and one further up at Cocklaw, to bar the English raiders

from entering the valley. The mill, the malt-kiln and the brew houses of the monks, all have passed away despite the powerful protection of St Mary. Of human handiwork in those distant ages only faint outlines remain …'

The placenames Hunedon and Hunum first appeared around 1160 and the more modern Parish of Hownam or Hounam, which is derived from them, lies directly south of Morebattle Parish, whilst Hounam village itself is approximately five miles south of Morebattle village. The origins of the name Hownam are obscure, but probably come from Houna, Howen or Owen and meant Hounas, Howens or Owens settlement, probably from the old Brythonic personal names coupled to the later Saxon ham meaning settlement. Like its neighbours, Hownam is a rural parish set amongst the northern slopes of the Cheviot hills and measuring some ten miles by six. As in many of the rural parishes of southern Scotland the population outside the main villages and towns has greatly diminished since the start of the eighteenth century, indeed when the first *statistical account* was written towards the end of that century the population had already nearly halved in the preceding forty years largely as a result of changes in agricultural practices.

The main settlement is Hownam itself, and though little more than a clachan, it once boasted two public houses - the Dicksons Arms Inn near the junction of the roads to Greenhill and Chatto and, slightly further north and amongst the main row of houses, the Shepherds Inn. The Shepherds Arms had gone by 1920 and the Dicksons Arms somehow lost its license in 1922 and is now a private house. The church and churchyard are to the north of the main row of houses and the village hall to the south and on the opposite side of the road.

The area is notable for its archeology. In the west of the parish the old Roman road of Dere Street, locally known as The Street runs basically from South to North on its journey from York to Trimontium (Melrose) and Perth and is flanked by the ancient Roman camps of Pennymuir. These camps – certainly three in number and possibly four – are said to be the best preserved Roman marching camps in Scotland. In 1948 Mrs C.M. Piggot excavated the celebrated Hownam Rings, a series of Iron Age earthworks and hut circles. Long known about and recognized, the Hownam Rings are mentioned by the Rev. George Rutherford in the *New Statistical Account* of 1836, but what was to excite the world of British archaeology was Piggot's discovery that these rings represented a series of occupations over a period of more than 500 years.

At one time Yetholm Loch extended from Marlefield in the west to beyond Linton Burnfoot in the east, though nature with some evident human assistance has reduced it greatly in size. At the north-east corner of what remains of Yetholm Loch stands the nineteenth century house and farm of Loch Tower. These two sets of buildings are built close to the site of the old Loch Tower which was razed by the Earl of Surrey on the night of 17 May 1523, as a part of his punitive cavalry and light artillery raids into the Borders during that year. These raids incorporated attacks on Jedburgh, Kelso, and much of the rest of the Borderland and formed a part of the long running Border Wars between England and Scotland. The original Loch Tower stood on an island in the loch, was accessed by a causeway and some say was the prototype for Sir Walter Scott's Border Keep in *The Monastery*, the tenth of his famous *Waverley* novels. This early twentieth century postcard was sent as a New Year card to a family in Alwinton, Rothbury, Northumberland.

This photograph shows the twin villages of Kirk Yetholm (in the middle distance) and Town Yetholm (in the near distance to the right) and seems to have been taken from the flank of Venchen Hill. Brooding over the villages is Staraugh – or Staerough – Hill.

A photograph of Kirk Yetholm's Green, taken from the entrance to the village from Main Street. The white building at the far end of the green is now the Border Hotel, which was seriously damaged by fire in the remaining thatched roof on 8 June 2006. The hotel is particularly well known to walkers as it marks the end of the Pennine Way and has been used by thousands to slake their thirst at the end of that exhilarating but exhausting trek.

A similar view to the previous photograph but taken rather earlier. The view looks totally different because it was taken from a point closer to the church and the single storey houses on the left of the picture obscure any view of the two storey examples which stand further back from the road and closer to the green. In addition the Border Hotel, in the distance, has its distinctive gable missing. Built in 1750, originally as coaching inn, it was first named the 'Grey Horse' and is marked as such on the Ordnance Survey map of 1859. In 1893 the thatched roof of the main building was replaced and it became the Old Border Hotel; then in 1898 the extra 'half timbered' gable was added and since then it has been known as the 'Border Hotel'. All of this dates the photograph to before 1893.

An early twentieth century view of Kirk Yetholm's High Street, formerly known as Gypsyland, Muggers Row or Tinkers Row. The present Gypsy Palace stands at the top of the row of houses on the right-hand side in this view looking up Staerough Hill from the Green. Its predecessor stood on the opposite side of the road and rather closer to the camera.

Above: The Gypsy Palace is a modest building, distinguished only by being detached and was formerly the home for some years to the Gypsy King and Queen. It is little changed from those years although a modern garage has since been built next to it.

Left: Queen Esther Faa-Blythe was the last of the 'Royal Faas' and reigned from 1861 to 1883. She is universally acclaimed as having been a highly intelligent and extremely shrewd woman and much attached to the clay pipes through which she took her tobacco. She married John Rutherford (Jethart Jock) in an irregular marriage at Coldstream and lived in the Gypsy Palace on Muggers Row. In 1866 a writer called George Borrow visited her and recorded that '...there was something of the gentlewoman in her.' Visited in 1880 by Joseph Lucas (author of *The Yetholm History of the Gypsies* in 1882), he remarked that '...she was distinguished by a dignity of bearing and a courteous independence...' Sadly, for all these gifts, in 1867 she was offered a place in Jedburgh Poor House, which is presumably where Lucas met her. She died on 12 July 1883 in Kelso, but was buried at Kirk Yetholm among her own people.

The seventy-three year old Charles Faa-Blythe II, 'King of the Yetholm Gypsies', and his attendants at his 'Coronation' on 30 May 1898. Real name Charles Rutherford, he was the son of Esther Faa-Blythe and John Rutherford, better known as Jethart Jock. On his mother's death in 1883 Charles returned home from England but it was some years before he agreed to take the vacant 'Royal' title. The fact that he was crowned at all seems to owe much to the new minister, the Rev. William Carrick Miller, who was installed that same year. The local population certainly took the occasion to their hearts and many dressed up for the occasion. The *Hawick News* carried a report that 'Several prominent [people] were present, including Lady Stratheden and Campbell, and Sir George Douglas. The succession was not without dispute because a letter was read out by the minister from William Blythe of Edinburgh, the son of David Blythe of Chirnside, who was in turn the son of David Blythe, Queen Esther's older brother. In the event neither William nor David turned up at Yetholm to dispute the event and so the Coronation proceeded amid scenes of great ribaldry.'

It was in July/August 1907 that Lieutenant-General Robert Baden-Powell took his party of twenty or so boy scouts to Brownsea Island off the coast of Poole, Dorset. That experimental camp was a great success and was soon emulated up and down the country. Even though the rapid growth of the movement was internationally acclaimed, it must have been something of a surprise to the villagers of Kirk Yetholm when the Berwick-upon-Tweed scouts arrived in 1914 to camp above Muggers Row, for nothing like it had ever been seen in the area before.

Physical fitness was very much in vogue at this time, not least to help beat the scourge of tuberculosis, and nowhere more so than in the Scout movement. Here a display of physical exercises is undertaken by the scouts and quite a throng of local people has assembled to watch the display.

Celebrations took place on 22 May 1911 for the coronation of King George V throughout the United Kingdom, and Yetholm was no exception. These were the days before television and widespread travel and any occasion for genuine celebration was seized upon. Here we see the start of the procession from Kirk Yetholm as the accompanied children, waving their Union flags and Scottish Royal Standards, march down the Mill Brae on their way to Town Yetholm and lunch.

It's not only the piper who looks a little fatigued as the assembled throng marches back up the Mill Brae to Kirk Yetholm at the end of a long and tiring day. The mill from which the Mill Brae took its name is on the right. A traditional corn mill, fortunately much of its fabric remains and is currently undergoing a metamorphosis into a tea room. As in other cases of mills on the Beaumont Water, the lade and water wheel, together with the associated machinery, have long since disappeared.

About a mile south-south-west of Kirk Yetholm, and nearly halfway to Primside Mill, is Duncanhaugh Mill. It dates from the late eighteenth century and in its original incarnation was a flour and corn mill. In the late 1990s it was converted into a dwelling and is now used for holiday accommodation.

Horses and carts prepare to take the residents of Town Yetholm on their outing to Spittal, near Berwick-upon-Tweed. In the early days the trip was undertaken by horse and cart to Mindrum Station on the North Eastern Railway's Alnwick and Cornhill Branch and thence by train to Coldstream Station at Cornhill, from where the train would take them to Berwick and on to Spittal. In later years motor coaches made such journeys easier and a few times forays were made as far as Dunbar. But Spittal remained the favourite and the villagers always returned there. The advent of the motor car with the consequent increase in mobility led to a decline in the popularity of these trips for which the school children got a day off, but the trips didn't finally end until the 1990s. They originated before the advent of the railways to enable local people to travel occasionally outside their immediate district and see a little of the world, though exactly when they started is obscure.

The visit of a photographer, not least a female one, would have been an unusual occurrence in the early 1900s. The occasion was probably a hunt gathering judging by the booted gentleman talking to a lady in the middle ground. Behind the motor car can be seen two boys already mounted and ready for the chase. The obelisk in the center of the picture is often mistaken for the war memorial but is in fact a memorial to Major-General Andrew Wauchope, who was killed leading the Highland Brigade at the Battle of Magersfontein in December 1899. The Wauchope family had a long association with Town Yetholm as landowners.

This photograph was probably taken immediately after the one on the previous page and shows the hunt having gathered around the Wauchope Memorial. The ages and attires of the various riders give a good indication that hunting was very much an activity enjoyed by the whole community, although few, if any, females took part.

A view of the entrance to Nichol's market garden which was located on the south side of Morebattle Road, Town Yetholm. The thatched roof of the cottage was once fairly typical of Border houses of this type but nowadays most have been replaced by slate, or even tiles, though in this case neither the house nor the shed beyond it exist any longer. The entrance to the market garden was between the two buildings, where the cart stands. The Nichols, father and son, ran the market garden here for many years; it finally closed in 1979 on the death of Robert Nichol who was also a local joiner. The area of land taken up by the market garden, owned by the Wauchope family, continues to be used by villagers as gardens or allotments. In the left foreground can be seen a 'pant', or well, from which the water supply would have been taken. Some of these still exist around the village, though this one disappeared along with the house.

On the north side of the Morebattle Road, Town Yetholm, stands Romany House which was completed in 1900 for Dr and Mrs Rodgers. A second doctor then occupied it before it changed hands once again and became a hotel. It appears to be around this time that the building was given the name 'Romany House', but it has no known connection with the Kirk Yetholm Gypsies. Having taken a turn as a nursing home, nowadays this fine, B-listed, Italianate villa is run by Mrs S. Keddie as a bed and breakfast and it is particularly popular with walkers on the Pennine Way and St Cuthbert's Way.

Town Yetholm's St James's Church was first built in 1786 and then pulled down and rebuilt on the same site in 1882. Over the years from 1815, the various secession churches re-combined and by 1914 were using St James's. However, in 1940 this church combined with Kirk Yetholm Parish Church at Kirk Yetholm and was closed. It was sold in 1954 and is now used for storage.

A view from around 1920 of the south-west end of Town Yetholm, looking towards the Green. Two of the houses pictured still have thatched roofs and the provision of street lamps is somewhat spartan by modern standards.

A 1920s view of the houses and businesses facing the Green in Town Yetholm, with W. Hardie's shop on the left and the Plough Inn further along the row. The house next to Hardie's is still thatched today.

The north-east end of Town Yetholm, looking down the High Street and showing the Green. The signpost in the distance indicates that the left turn leads to Kelso while straight on is the road to Coldstream by way of Venchen and Mindrum. Just out of this shot a right turn leads down Dow Brae to Beaumont Water and then to Kirk Yetholm.

The motor car had started to impinge on the streets by the time this photograph was taken in the 1920s. An early garage or motor house, as they were often called in those days, is visible in the left foreground and the road had by then received a MacAdam surface.

Situated about a mile north-north-east of Town Yetholm, hard by the side of the B6352 road, stand the Venchen Cottages. In the past these were used to accommodate farm workers from Venchen Farm, about half a mile to the west, as well as those working in the quarry which can just be made out in the background between the two left-hand, detached, houses. Today the houses in this early twentieth century photograph still stand, the nearest on the left being occupied while the other detached house has been abandoned. The row of cottages on the roadside have been converted from four to two. While all the cottages still belong to Venchen Farm, the quarry has ceased to be operational.

This postcard was sent on 16 October 1926 to a Miss Doris Hall of Felling-on-Tyne and depicts two young men whiling away some time on the Quarry Brig at Morebattle. A bridge still exists at this point over the Kale Water, near to the site of Grubet Mill, about half a mile east-south-east of Morebattle, and now forms an integral part of the public path known as St Cuthbert's Way.

The building off-centre served as Morebattle's school from 1873, under the care first of a Mr Henderson (headmaster) and then of Mr Donald Craig until 1931. Mr Craig oversaw the transfer of the school into its new building in 1931. The building was purchased by the villagers when it ceased to be used by the Education Authority and was used for a while as the Young Men's Club before being taken over as a village institute, still used today by local groups for meetings and fund-raising events.

Teapot St. Morebattle

Morebattle's Teapot Street. A name much admired, or at least commented on, it is thought to have arisen from a corruption of 'Tip It' Street and indeed it was the site of the village tip or midden. At the very far end of the street, out of site in this view, there was a ford over the River Kale then a path to Morebattle Tofts and Thornyhaugh. In the furthest of the right-hand single-storey buildings was the village smithy. At various times Teapot Street and Well Brae, the continuation that led down to the Kale, also contained a builder's yard, a slaughterhouse, a gamekeeper's premises, a haulier's, a bakehouse and a grocer's shop.

In the days before the now-obligatory 'sheep dip' it was standard practice for a 'sheep washing' to take place before shearing. In part, this was aimed at removing nits from the fleece but more practically and more effectively it was a means of getting rid of the grit and dust which could blunt the shears of the shearers. They were usually driven into the water in groups of twenty or thirty at a time by a combination of men and dogs. In this photograph the old ford on the Bowmont Water by Mowhaugh School is being used while some intrepid pupils watch. The 'sheep washing' was a popular occasion, usually witnessed by as many folk as could make themselves available to see it.

The spectators having left, one man and a dog continue the operation of driving the sheep into Bowmont Water under the watchful eye of either the 'farm steward' or possibly the farmer himself.

From the opposite bank to that seen on the previous pages, the children of Mowhaugh School watch attentively as the sodden sheep struggle ashore. Often during a 'sheep washing' it was necessary for one or two men to stand in the river to ensure that each sheep at some point became totally immersed. From the evidence of these pictures, it appears not to have been necessary on this occasion and certainly it was never popular work. Typically, it would involve standing in the water for four or five hours, up-turning each animal to ensure total immersion. An individual could only be expected to perform such work for four or five years and afterward many who did it suffered with arthritis. Though the 'washing' tended to be conducted in June, the water running off the high slopes of the Cheviots would be very cold indeed.

Above: Mowhaugh School was built in 1833 and even though at one time it had a hundred scholars it became one of the earliest rural school closures in the district. It must have been difficult to attract a new teacher to the school in view of the fact that that the wage paid to the schoolmistress was half that paid the schoolmaster at Morebattle. In the New Year of 1945 the teacher at Mowhaugh was taken ill and before she was able to return to work the school was closed and the children taken to Town Yetholm School.

Opposite: It is likely that the lady standing is the schoolmistress of Mowhaugh School as she is photographed with the pupils, and the horse, above and on the front cover. They were posing on the riverbank below Mowhaugh School at exactly the same spot as the 'sheep washing' took place.

About a quarter of a mile north-west of Mowhaugh stood the farm and settlement of Belford, which can just be made out between the trees. In the foreground is the footbridge which served the path linking the two communities. To the right of this picture stood the ancient 'Tower' of Mow or Molle, which was destroyed along with its inhabitants by the English Border Warden, Sir William Eure, in 1546. Near Belford stood the *circa* twelfth century parish church of Mow or Molle, no longer in existence. It was probably initially abandoned, then allowed to fall into disrepair and crumble. Thereafter, the stones would have been used by local people to build dykes, sheep stells, and dwellings. The parish of Mow was abolished in 1672, at a time when the Kirk was finding it hard to recruit ministers; the last recorded minister of the parish was Robert Martin, who served from 1617 to 1618. The former parish of Mow or Molle now forms the southernmost part of the parish of Morebattle. Only some old gravestones now mark the site of Mow Church.

A view of Primsidemill, which lies about three miles upstream (south) of Kirk Yetholm on the Bowmont water, showing the Primside mill itself in the left foreground and its associated accommodation behind. The mill was a corn mill, one of many in the area in the nineteenth century. The stone bridge toward the right of the picture carries the road to Clifton. All the buildings in the foreground of that road, including the mill, are now demolished though those on the far side remain.

This is the single row of houses that largely constitutes Hownam village, high up in the Cheviot Hills and looking towards Morebattle.

HOWNAM.

The Georgian mansion of Greenhill stands around two miles south-east of Hownam, near the confluence of the Heatherhope and Capelhope Burns. Originally built as a shooting lodge for the Duke of Roxburghe, it was used between 1940 and 1943 by the Rudolph Steiner School, which had been evacuated from Edinburgh. It has now been transformed into luxurious self-catering accommodation for up to sixteen people.

The Yetholm Border Shepherds' Show had by 2005 been staged on 148 occasions in its 160 year history; in the other 12 years it was not held for reasons of flood, war and disease. The show continues to be staged every October.

Yetholm Border Shepherds' Show.
Saturday, October 20, 1906.

HALF-BRED LAMB.

First Prize

A winning ticket from the Yetholm Border Shepherds' Show of 1906. This particular ticket was awarded to the best 'half-bred' lamb in the show. 'Half-bred' at that time meant a crossbred Border Leicester-Cheviot animal.

Yetholm Border Shepherds' Show.
Saturday, October 17, 1908.

Hirsel Sheep (Dressed)

Second Prize

In 1908 this ticket was awarded for the second-best 'dressed' hirsel sheep in the show. A 'hirsel sheep' was one from a shepherd's own flock – in those days and for many years afterward it was normal for a shepherd to be allowed by his employer, as part of his stipend, to maintain a flock of his own. Dressed in this sense means prepared – the fleece would be washed and combed, the feet fettled and polished, the teeth and gums cleaned, etc.

Yetholm Border Shepherds' Show.
Saturday, October 19, 1907.

2 Half-bred Ewes (1 and 2 crop)

Second Prize

The original owner of this ticket won Second Prize for two half-bred ewes in the 1907 Shepherds' Show. The expression 'half-bred' once again relates to cross-bred Border Leicester-Cheviot sheep, while a pair was demanded with the intention of demonstrating that such animals were produced with at least a little consistency.

❋ **YETHOLM** ❋
Border Shepherds' Show.
SATURDAY, 9th OCTOBER, 1920.

First Prize.

Most prestigious of all was the award for 'First Prize'. This was awarded to the very finest exhibit in the show within the livestock category and carried with it automatic qualification for the winner to enter the Royal Highland Show.

Agricultural shows were the highlight of the year right across the Borders in largely agricultural communities such as Yetholm. For the shepherds they were also anxious occasions because the reputation of a shepherd, or even that of a farm, could be enhanced or gravely damaged by the condition of the animals put on show.

Dancers from the Walmsley Troupe entertain the crowds at the 1913 Yetholm Shepherds' Show. All of this additional entertainment helped to produce the festive atmosphere which accompanied agricultural shows throughout the Borders in the early twentieth century.

A fine array of turnips, or neeps, at the 1911 Shepherds' Show. The importance of turnips gradually waned during the twentieth century and substantial displays like this gradually disappeared from the shows. In the years when turnips were an important crop for animal and human feed, many women, often bondagers, were employed at the 'shawin' or cutting off of the stalks and leaves of the turnips. This was undertaken in the fields and was back-breaking work.

The sheepdog was a prize possession amongst the shepherds and though they were worked hard they were treated well; typically a working dog was fed before his master! Here we see about a dozen Border Collie sheepdogs tethered to stakes driven into the ground for the purpose of exhibition. Often sheepdog trials were held in conjunction with the shows and at these the dogs' working talents were assessed by a panel of judges while the shepherds instructed them to carry out a series of manoeuvres with a small flock of sheep.

In the days before the advent of widespread motor transport the horse and cart was essential to everyday life. If something or somebody needed to be taken anything more than a very short distance this was the only means of doing it, at least as far as the nearest railway station. It was therefore important that both were well maintained. For extra special occasions the rig would be 'dressed' and one such occasion was the Shepherds' Show. Here we see an array of horses and carts which have been so 'dressed': carts cleaned, perhaps even treated to a lick of paint, horses lovingly groomed, tack and harnesses polished, and burnished horse brasses gleaming in the sunlight.

For those who were less concerned, or perhaps less directly involved, with the serious business of sheep, cattle and agricultural produce, entertainment at the Yetholm Shepherds' Show was provided by pipe bands like this one pictured at the 1913 event.

Its duties over for the time being, the band relax along with the crowd. At least one bandsman is enjoying a clay pipe, and in this picture all eyes are on something taking place to the left while the horses and their drivers, on the right, await the visit of the judges.

While the older men study the sheep intently, a group of ladies on the left of the photograph obviously find a 'guid blather' more to their taste. The two boys in the centre are more interested in the photographer's activities.